VISHWAMITRA

ONCE, LONG AGO, WHILE ROAMING OVER THE EARTH WITH HIS HUNDRED SONS AND VAST ARMIES, THE MIGHTY KING VISHWAMITRA CAME UPON THE HERMITAGE OF THE POWERFUL SAGE VASISHTHA.

IT IS SURPRIS— ING, BUT THE SIGHT OF THESE ASCETICS WHO HAVE RENOUNCED THE WORLD EXHILA— RATES ME.

* MAHA RISHI

1

VISHWAMITRA WALKED UP TO VASISHTHA.

I BOW MY HEAD AT YOUR FEET.

WELCOME O KING. COME, SIT DOWN. I PRESUME ALL IS WELL IN YOUR KINGDOM.

VISHWAMITRA SAT NEAR THE SAGE AND THEY TALKED OF MANY THINGS. THEN —

I WISH TO HONOUR YOU AND YOUR ROYAL RETINUE. PLEASE LET ME BE THE HOST AT A BANQUET WORTHY OF YOU.

O WISE SAGE, THE VERY SIGHT OF YOU IS A PRIVILEGE AND THIS GRACIOUS WELCOME, AN HONOUR. PRAY PERMIT US TO DEPART NOW.

I INSIST THAT YOU BE THE GUESTS AT MY FEAST.

WE WILL STAY, SINCE IT IS YOUR WISH.

THEREUPON VASISHTHA SENT FOR HIS FAVOURITE COW, THE DIVINE KAMADHENU.*

DEAR KAMADHENU, PROVIDE US WITH FOOD FIT FOR A GREAT KING.

*THE WISH - FULFILLING

2

IN AN INSTANT, THERE EMERGED FROM THE DIVINE COW, CHOICE FOOD FOR THE ROYAL VISITORS.

VISHWAMITRA AND HIS MEN ATE TO THEIR HEART'S CONTENT.

I HAVE NEVER TASTED SUCH DELICACIES BEFORE. KAMADHENU SHOULD BELONG TO ME!

WHEN THE FEAST WAS OVER —

KAMADHENU IS A JEWEL AND JEWELS BELONG TO THE KING. BY RIGHT SHE SHOULD BE MINE. YET I WILL GIVE YOU A HUNDRED THOUSAND MILCH COWS IN RETURN.

NO. I CANNOT PART WITH HER EVEN FOR 1,00,00,000 COWS.

VASISHTHA'S REFUSAL MADE VISHWAMITRA'S DESIRE KEENER. HE INCREASED HIS PRICE.

I WILL GIVE YOU 14,000 ELEPHANTS HARNESSED AND CAPARISONED IN GOLD, 800 CHARIOTS OF SOLID GOLD EACH DRAWN BY FOUR MILK-WHITE HORSES, 11,000 THOROUGHBRED HORSES ALSO HARNESSED IN GOLD AND 10 MILLION COWS OF VARIOUS HUES. ALL THIS AND AS MUCH GOLD AS YOU WANT, SHALL BE YOURS. GIVE ME KAMADHENU.

BUT VASISHTHA TURNED DOWN THE OFFER.

FOR NO TREASURE ON EARTH WILL I PART WITH HER, O KING. SHE IS THE VERY SOURCE OF MY SPIRITUAL LIFE. SHE PROVIDES ME WITH ALL I NEED FOR MY RITUALS.

THEN I SHALL HAVE TO TAKE HER AWAY BY FORCE.

VISHWAMITRA CALLED TO HIS MEN.

SEIZE THE SAGE'S COW OF PLENTY AND BRING HER TO ME.

THE KING'S MEN FELL UPON THE BEWILDERED KAMADHENU.

WHY DOES THE HOLY ONE PERMIT THIS OUTRAGE? I HAVE ALWAYS LOVED AND SERVED HIM! I WILL SHAKE OFF MY TORMENTORS AND GO TO HIM.

KAMADHENU TOSSED ASIDE HER CAPTORS...

...AND FLED.

SHE STOOD BEFORE VASISHTHA, WEEPING AND LOWING.

O LORD, HAVE YOU FORSAKEN ME? DID YOU NOT SEE HOW I WAS TREATED?

DEAR ONE, I AM HELPLESS AGAINST THE KING AND HIS MIGHTY ARMY.

KAMADHENU WAS NOT CONVINCED.

YOUR SPIRITUAL POWERS ARE DIVINE AND BOUNDLESS. HIS MORTAL STRENGTH IS GREAT BUT LIMITED. O HOLY ONE, COMMAND ME AND BY YOUR LIMITLESS SPIRITUAL POWERS I SHALL HUMBLE THE PRIDE OF THIS WICKED WARRIOR.

SO BE IT, KAMADHENU.

SO KAMADHENU LOWED LOUD AND LONG. HORDES AND HORDES OF WARRIORS SPRANG UP MIRACULOUSLY AND CHARGED AT THE KING'S SOLDIERS...

...AND SOON DESTROYED THEM.

ENRAGED, THE SONS OF VISHWAMITRA RUSHED TOWARDS VASISHTHA.

THE SAGE STOOD FIRM AND CALM. HE UTTERED BUT ONE SYLLABLE...

HMM..M.M

...THE MERE SOUND OF WHICH BURNT THE PRINCES AND THEIR HORSES, CHARIOTS, WEAPONS AND ALL.

NOW I HAVE BUT THE ONE SON WHO STAYED BACK TO RULE THE KINGDOM.

VISHWAMITRA RETURNED TO HIS KINGDOM FULL OF GRIEF AND SHAME. THERE —

MY SON, THE KINGDOM IS YOURS. RULE VIRTU- OUSLY OVER IT. I PLAN TO RETIRE TO THE FORESTS FOR A WHILE.

HE WENT STRAIGHT TO THE HIMALAYAS AND BEGAN PRACTIS- ING SEVERE AUSTERITIES

I SHALL PROPI- TIATE LORD SHIVA AND BY HIS GRACE AVENGE THE DEATH OF MY GLORIOUS SONS.

AT LAST SHIVA WAS PLEASED. HE STOOD BEFORE VISHWAMITRA.

THE BOON THAT YOU SEEK O KING, SHALL BE YOURS.

BY YOUR GRACE, LET ALL KNOWLEDGE OF WEAPONS AND WARFARE BE MINE.

SHIVA GRANTED THE BOON AND WENT BACK TO HIS ABODE.

A TRIUMPHANT VISHWAMITRA NOW TURNED HIS FOOTSTEPS TOWARDS VASISHTHA'S HERMITAGE.

MERCY, O KING. MERCY.

AS SOON AS VISHWAMITRA REACHED THE HERMITAGE HE SENT OUT FLAMING MISSILES AND SET IT ABLAZE.

RUN!

RUN!

THIS HERMITAGE IS NO LONGER A HAVEN FOR THE HOLY.

VASISHTHA TRIED TO STOP THEM, BUT IN VAIN.

WAIT. DO NOT RUN AWAY. I WILL DESTROY THE EVIL KING.

A DEADLY SILENCE DESCENDED OVER THE DESERTED HERMITAGE. IT WAS BROKEN BY THE RESONANT VOICE OF VASISHTHA.

WICKED, DELUDED ONE. YOU HAVE WANTONLY DESTROYED MY ANCIENT HERMITAGE. FOR THIS YOU SHALL DIE.

SNATCHING HIS STAFF HE ADVANCED TOWARDS VISHWAMITRA.

BEWARE! MY WEAPONS WILL CONSUME YOU.

EVIL WARRIOR, LET US SEE HOW YOUR WEAPONS OF DESTRUCTION ENCOUNTER SPIRITUAL POWER.

VISHWAMITRA HURLED THE WEAPON. BUT —

ADMIT NOW, THE IMPOTENCE OF ALL YOUR WEAPONS.

VISHWAMITRA IN DESPERATION HURLED WEAPON, AFTER...

...WEAPON.

BUT THEY WERE ALL ABSORBED BY VASISHTHA'S STAFF.

AT LAST VISHWAMITRA SENT OUT THE FATAL BRAHMASTRA. BUT...

...VASISHTHA SUBDUED EVEN THAT.

VISHWAMITRA, HIS PRIDE HUMBLED, HAD TO ADMIT DEFEAT.

THE MIGHT OF A WARRIOR IS USELESS. SPIRITUAL POWER IS THE GREATEST POWER OF ALL. I SHALL REALISE BRAHMAN AND THE STATUS OF BRAHMARSHI!*

HE LAID DOWN HIS ARMS AND WENT HOME TO HIS QUEEN.

I WANT TO BECOME A BRAHMARSHI. WE SHALL GO TO A HERMITAGE IN THE SOUTH. THERE YOU WILL HELP ME IN MY PENANCES.

AS YOU COMMAND, MY LORD.

SO VISHWAMITRA AND HIS QUEEN SET OUT. THEY REACHED THE CHOSEN HERMITAGE AND...

THIS TIME I SHALL SEEK THE FAVOUR OF BRAHMA.

...VISHWAMITRA BEGAN HIS PENANCES. IN THAT PERIOD FOUR VIRTUOUS AND MIGHTY SONS WERE BORN TO HIM.

* BRAHMA RISHI.

THEN VISHWAMITRA CONTINUED HIS AUSTERITIES WITH GREATER SEVERITY UNTIL BRAHMA HAD TO APPEAR BEFORE HIM.

YOU ARE THE GREATEST ASCETIC AMONG KINGS. I CONFER UPON YOU THE STATUS OF RAJARSHI*

THE STATUS OF MERE RAJARSHI IS NO REWARD FOR THE PENANCES I HAVE UNDERGONE. I SHALL ASK FOR ...

BUT BRAHMA HAD ALREADY DEPARTED. VISHWAMITRA WAS DEJECTED.

IN SPITE OF ALL MY PENANCES I AM ONLY A RAJARSHI TO THE GODS. I WILL STRIVE HARDER FOR GREATER SPIRITUAL POWERS.

MEANWHILE TRISHANKU, A GREAT KING OF THOSE TIMES, WAS SUDDENLY SEIZED WITH AN AMBITION.

I WILL ENTER HEAVEN IN MY MORTAL BODY. I SHALL ASK MY GURU, VASISHTHA, TO HELP ME PERFORM A SACRIFICE TO ACHIEVE THIS.

HE SENT FOR VASISHTHA.

I WISH TO ENTER HEAVEN IN THIS MORTAL FRAME OF MINE, SO...

NO! O KING! THAT CAN NEVER BE!

* RAJA RISHI

13

BUT TRISHANKU REFUSED TO GIVE UP THE IDEA.

IF MY GURU WILL NOT HELP ME, HIS SONS WILL. I SHALL GO TO THEIR HERMITAGE IN THE SOUTH.

THERE TRISHANKU TOLD THE SONS OF VASISHTHA OF THEIR FATHER'S DECISION.

PRAY, WILL **YOU** BECOME MY GURUS AND HELP ME?

HOW DARE YOU SEEK OUR AID WHEN YOUR GURU, OUR WISE FATHER, HAS DISAPPROVED. YOU ARE NOT FIT TO CLAIM HIM AS YOUR GURU, YOU IGNORANT ONE.

BUT TRISHANKU WAS BENT UPON PERFORMING THE SACRIFICE.

THEN I SHALL HAVE TO SEEK THE HELP OF SOME OTHER SAGE.

THE SONS OF VASISHTHA WERE FURIOUS WITH THE ADAMANT KING.

O EVIL KING, MAY YOU BECOME A CHANDALA.*

TO HIS DISMAY TRISHANKU FOUND HIS BODY TRANSFORMED.

ALAS! ALAS! WHAT HAVE I, A VIRTUOUS KING, DONE TO DESERVE THIS? WHICH SAGE WILL HELP ME NOW, OUTCASTE AS I AM?

THEN SUDDENLY, HE REMEMBERED VISHWAMITRA.

I WILL GO TO THE RAJARSHI. HE WILL HELP ME.

AS HE EXPECTED, VISHWAMITRA RECEIVED HIM COMPASSIONATELY AND LISTENED TO HIS TALE OF WOE.

O HOLY SAGE, APART FROM YOU THERE IS NONE I CAN TURN TO. I BESEECH YOU, HELP ME OUT OF THIS PLIGHT.

* AN OUTCASTE

VISHWAMITRA CONSOLED AND COMFORTED THE MISERABLE KING.

YOU ARE A VIRTUOUS PERSON. I WILL HELP YOU PERFORM THE SACRIFICE. YOU WILL ENTER HEAVEN AND IN THIS VERY FORM WHICH YOUR GURU'S SONS HAVE IMPOSED ON YOU.

VISHWAMITRA SUMMONED HIS SONS TO HIM.

MAKE ALL ARRANGEMENTS FOR THE SACRIFICE.

NEXT VISHWAMITRA CALLED HIS DISCIPLES TO HIM.

INVITE ALL THE PIOUS AND THE LEARNED OF THE LAND HERE FOR THE GREAT SACRIFICE.

THE DISCIPLES RETURNED AFTER A FEW DAYS.

SAGE VASISHTHA AND HIS SONS REFUSE TO COME. THE SONS SAY THEY WOULD BE DEFILED.*

MAY THEY BE DESTROYED FOR DISREGARDING ONE WHO IS A SAGE AND FREE OF GUILT.

* ASSOCIATING ONESELF WITH UNTOUCHABLES MADE ONE UNCLEAN.

16

WHEN THOSE WHO HAD ACCEPTED THE INVITATION ASSEMBLED—

THIS VIRTUOUS KING SEEKS YOUR GOODWILL FOR THIS SACRIFICE IN A NOBLE PURSUIT.

THEN THE RITES BEGAN, WITH VISHWAMITRA OFFICIATING AS THE CHIEF PRIEST.

WHEN THE RITES WERE OVER—

O DEVAS*, COME YE FROM THE HEAVENS. ACCEPT THESE OFFERINGS AND LEAD THIS GREAT KING TO HEAVEN IN HIS OWN BODY.

VISHWAMITRA WAITED. BUT NONE OF THE DEVAS APPEARED. HE WAS ENRAGED.

O KING, I WILL RAISE YOU TO HEAVEN ON THE STRENGTH OF ALL THE SPIRITUAL POWERS I HAVE ACCUMULATED.

VISHWAMITRA THEN LOOKED SKYWARDS.

MAY YOU ASCEND TO HEAVEN AS YOU ARE, O VIRTUOUS KING.

* GODS

17

HARDLY HAD VISHWAMITRA UTTERED THESE WORDS THAN THE ASCENSION OF TRISHANKU BEGAN.

BUT WHEN HE REACHED HEAVEN, INDRA AND THE DEVAS BARRED HIS ENTRY.

WRETCH! YOU HAVE BEEN CURSED BY YOUR GURU'S SONS. HEAVEN HAS NO PLACE FOR YOU. MAY YOU GO DOWN TO THE DEPTHS OF THE EARTH.

TRISHANKU BEGAN FALLING DOWN, DOWN —

SAVE ME! O HOLY ONE, SAVE ME!

VISHWAMITRA WOULD NOT ACCEPT DEFEAT.

MAY YOU STOP WHERE YOU ARE. I SHALL CREATE A HEAVEN AROUND YOU.

AND VISHWAMITRA CREATED SEVEN PLANETS, THE SAPTARSHIS* AND TWENTY-SEVEN STARS. BUT HE WAS NOT SATISFIED.

I WILL CREATE ANOTHER INDRA. OR BETTER STILL I WILL HURL INDRA OUT OF HEAVEN AND MAKE TRISHANKU THE KING OF THE DEVAS!

WHEN THE DEVAS DIVINED HIS INTENTIONS, THEY WERE PERTURBED.

WE MUST STOP HIM.

THEY APPEARED BEFORE HIM AND PLEADED WITH HIM.

O SAGE, THE KING HAS BEEN CURSED BY HIS GURU'S SONS. HOW CAN WE GIVE HIM A PLACE IN HEAVEN?

* SAPTA RISHI

19

BUT VISHWAMITRA WAS FIRM.

I HAVE PROMISED TO HELP HIM. LET HIM ENTER YOUR HEAVEN. LET THE PLANETS I HAVE CREATED EXIST AS LONG AS YOUR HEAVEN DOES. THEN INDRA SHALL REMAIN IN HEAVEN, THE SOLE KING OF THE DEVAS.

SO BE IT. TRISHANKU, SURROUNDED BY THE PLANETS THAT SHINE ON HIM, SHALL BECOME IMMORTAL AND REMAIN SUSPENDED IN HEAVEN, HEAD DOWNWARDS.

AS THE DEVAS, HEAVING SIGHS OF RELIEF, DEPARTED TO HEAVEN—

EVEN AS A RAJARSHI, VISHWAMITRA HAS HUMBLED US. WE MUST ENSURE THAT HE NEVER BECOMES A BRAHMARSHI.

I HAVE HUMBLED THE DEVAS BUT EXHAUSTED MY SPIRITUAL POWERS. I WILL START ALL OVER AGAIN.

20

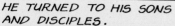

HE TURNED TO HIS SONS AND DISCIPLES.

THE WORLD HAS BEEN TOO MUCH WITH ME HERE. MY PENANCES HAVE COME TO NAUGHT. I SHALL GO WEST TO THE PEACEFUL PUSH-KAR TO RESUME MY PENANCES.

MEANWHILE AMBARISHA, KING OF AYODHYA, HAD DECIDED TO PERFORM A SACRIFICE. BUT —

YOUR MAJESTY, THE SACRIFICIAL ANIMAL HAS BEEN STOLEN.

AMBARISHA HUNTED FAR AND WIDE FOR THE ANIMAL. BUT AS INDRA WAS THE UNKNOWN THIEF HIS SEARCH WAS HOPELESS.

THE PRIEST GAVE HIM THE ONLY ALTERNATIVE.

YOU WILL HAVE TO PROVIDE A HUMAN VICTIM TO COMPLETE THE SACRI-FICE. OR ELSE GREAT HARM WILL BEFALL YOUR KINGDOM AND YOUR SUBJECTS.

AMBARISHA SET OUT AGAIN. HIS QUEST TOOK HIM THROUGH CITIES AND FORESTS TILL HE CAME UPON THE HERMITAGE WHERE RICHIKA LIVED WITH HIS WIFE AND SONS.

GREAT KING, WHAT BRINGS YOU TO OUR HUMBLE ABODE?

AMBARISHA TOLD HIM ALL.

O SAGE, GIVE ME ONE OF YOUR SONS FOR 100,000 COWS AND HELP ME COMPLETE THE SACRIFICE.

RICHIKA AND HIS WIFE LOOKED AT EACH OTHER.

I WILL NEVER GIVE UP MY ELDEST SON.

MY YOUNGEST SHALL EVER REMAIN WITH US.

SHUNAHSHEPA, THE MIDDLE SON, STEPPED FORWARD BEFORE HIS PARENTS COULD SAY MORE.

TAKE ME, THE MIDDLE SON, O KING, AND GIVE MY PARENTS 100,000 COWS.

DELIGHTED THAT HIS SEARCH HAD COME TO AN END, AMBARISHA TOOK SHUNAHSHEPA AND MOUNTING HIS CHARIOT TURNED HOMEWARD.

ON THE WAY THEY HAD TO PASS THROUGH THE FOREST OF PUSHKARA.

LET US REST FOR A WHILE AT THAT HERMITAGE OVER THERE.

AS THE KING RESTED, SHUNAHSHEPA WANDERED ABOUT THE HERMITAGE. SUDDENLY –

SAGE VISHWAMITRA, MY MOTHER'S BROTHER HERE!

SHUNAHSHEPA RAN TO HIM, FELL AT HIS FEET AND TOLD HIM ALL. THEN –

O HOLY ONE, I HAVE NEITHER FATHER NOR MOTHER. O LORD, PROTECT ME. LET ME LIVE, LEAD A SPIRITUAL LIFE AND ATTAIN HEAVEN.

BE CONSOLED, O VIRTUOUS SON. I WILL NOT LET YOU DIE.

VISHWAMITRA TURNED TO HIS SONS.

SHUNAHSHEPA HAS SOUGHT MY PROTECTION. ONE OF YOU TAKE HIS PLACE AND RESCUE HIM. I HAVE GIVEN HIM MY WORD. HELP ME KEEP IT.

O FATHER, WOULD YOU ABANDON ONE OF YOUR OWN SONS TO PROTECT ANOTHER'S?

YOU ARROGANT SONS. HAVE YOU NO AFFECTION FOR ME? MAY YOU LOSE YOUR CASTE AND WANDER ABOUT THE EARTH EATING THE FLESH OF DOGS.

VISHWAMITRA THEN ADDRESSED SHUNAHSHEPA.

I WILL TEACH YOU TWO MANTRAS IN PRAISE OF INDRA. REPEAT THEM AT THE SACRIFICIAL ALTAR AND YOU WILL BE SAVED.

SHUNAHSHEPA LEARNT THE MANTRAS AND RETURNED TO AMBARISHA.

O KING, LET US HASTEN TO THE SACRIFICIAL GROUND.

WHEN THEY REACHED THE SACRIFICIAL ALTAR, AMBA-RISHA HANDED SHUNAHSHEPA OVER TO THE PRIEST.

SHUNAHSHEPA REPEATED THE MANTRAS THAT VISHWAMITRA HAD TAUGHT HIM. SUDDENLY INDRA APPEARED BEFORE HIM.

I AM PLEASED WITH YOUR WOR-SHIP. MAY THE LONG LIFE YOU SEEK BE YOURS.

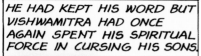

HE HAD KEPT HIS WORD BUT VISHWAMITRA HAD ONCE AGAIN SPENT HIS SPIRITUAL FORCE IN CURSING HIS SONS.

THIS TIME I WILL REMAIN HERE AND RESUME MY PENANCES.

ONE DAY WHILE HE WAS ON THE BANK OF THE PUSHKARA LAKE —

IT'S THE IRRESISTIBLE APSARA, MENAKA. I MUST MAKE HER MINE.

AS MENAKA CAME OUT OF THE LAKE, VISHWAMITRA DECLARED HIS LOVE TO HER.

I AM HONOURED, O VENERABLE SAGE.

A FEW YEARS PASSED BEFORE VISHWAMITRA SUDDENLY REALISED HIS FOLLY.

I SEE NOW! THE DEVAS MUST HAVE SENT YOU HERE TO DISTRACT ME.

MENAKA, AWARE OF THE SAGE'S FIERCE TEMPER, TREMBLED WITH FEAR. BUT THE SAGE WAS KIND TO HER.

GO BACK TO THE DEVAS, O APSARA. MAY YOU FARE WELL.

WHEN MENAKA LEFT —

I SHALL GO TO THE HIMALAYAS AND PERFORM MY PENANCES ON THE BANKS OF THE KAUSHIKI RIVER.

26

WHEN BRAHMA DEPARTED, VISHWAMITRA INTENSIFIED HIS AUSTERITIES.

IN SUMMER HE STOOD ON ONE FOOT IN THE MIDST OF FIVE BLAZING FIRES, LIVING ONLY ON AIR.

THROUGH THE RAINY SEASON HE CONTINUED STANDING.

AND IN WINTER HE STOOD IN THE MIDDLE OF A COLD STREAM.

THE DEVAS WERE ONCE AGAIN PERTURBED. THEN INDRA HAD AN IDEA.

I WILL ASK THE APSARA RAMBHA OF MY COURT TO DISTRACT HIM.

HE SENT FOR RAMBHA.

YOU MUST ATTRACT MAHARSHI VISHWA-MITRA AND DISTURB HIS PENANCES.

LORD, PLEASE DO NOT SEND ME ON THIS TASK. THE SAGE HAS A TERRIBLE TEMPER AND A READY CURSE.

BUT INDRA REASSURED HER.

DO NOT WORRY, RAMBHA. I WILL TAKE THE FORM OF A CUCKOO AND WILL SIT ON A BRANCH NEAR BY. GO, ADORN YOURSELF.

AS SOON AS RAMBHA WAS READY, THEY CAME TO VISHWAMITRA'S GROVE.

I WILL ROUSE HIM WITH MY NOTES. THAT IS THE MOMENT FOR YOU TO APPROACH HIM.

INDRA BEGAN WARBLING. RAMBHA WALKED TOWARDS VISHWAMITRA.

WHAT HEAVENLY NOTES!

VISHWAMITRA OPENED HIS EYES.

RAMBHA OF INDRA'S COURT? HERE? THIS IS ONE OF INDRA'S TRICKS.

VISHWAMITRA'S RAGE ONCE AGAIN GOT THE BETTER OF HIM.

RAMBHA, FOR THIS IMPERTINENCE MAY YOU BE TURNED INTO ROCK. SO YOU SHALL REMAIN FOR 10,000 YEARS TILL A BRAHMAN COMES AND DELIVERS YOU.

WHEN HE HEARD THIS, INDRA FLED FROM THE SCENE.

ONCE AGAIN MY SPIRITUAL FORCE HAS BEEN CONSUMED BY ANGER. I WILL NEITHER EAT, SPEAK NOR BREATHE TILL I HAVE CONQUERED THIS PASSION.

29

VISHWAMITRA WENT EASTWARD AND BEGAN HIS MOST SEVERE AUSTERITIES. WHEN HE WAS SURE THAT HE HAD CONQUERED ANGER—

I HAVE SUCCEEDED. I SHALL FIRST BREAK MY LONG FAST.

AS VISHWAMITRA SAT DOWN TO EAT—

O HOLY SAGE, I AM HUNGRY.

IT WAS INDRA WHO HAD COME IN THE GUISE OF A BRAHMAN TO TEST HIM. VISHWAMITRA WITHOUT UTTERING A WORD OFFERED HIM THE FOOD.

AFTER YEARS OF FURTHER PENANCE, THE TERRIBLE POWERS AMASSED BY VISHWAMITRA BEGAN TO EMIT PERVASIVE THICK SMOKE, STRIKING TERROR AMONG THE BEINGS OF THE THREE WORLDS.

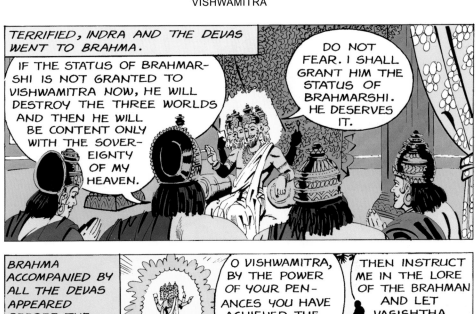

TERRIFIED, INDRA AND THE DEVAS WENT TO BRAHMA.

IF THE STATUS OF BRAHMAR-SHI IS NOT GRANTED TO VISHWAMITRA NOW, HE WILL DESTROY THE THREE WORLDS AND THEN HE WILL BE CONTENT ONLY WITH THE SOVER-EIGNTY OF MY HEAVEN.

DO NOT FEAR. I SHALL GRANT HIM THE STATUS OF BRAHMARSHI. HE DESERVES IT.

BRAHMA ACCOMPANIED BY ALL THE DEVAS APPEARED BEFORE THE SAGE.

O VISHWAMITRA, BY THE POWER OF YOUR PEN-ANCES YOU HAVE ACHIEVED THE STATUS OF BRAHMARSHI.

THEN INSTRUCT ME IN THE LORE OF THE BRAHMAN AND LET VASISHTHA ACKNOWLEDGE MY PRESENT STATUS.

THE GODS LED VASISHTHA TO VISHWAMITRA.

MY GREETINGS TO YOU, O BRAHMARSHI.

VISHWAMITRA TOO PAID HOMAGE TO VASISHTHA. THEN, HAVING ACHIEVED WHAT HE HAD SET OUT TO ACHIEVE, VISHWAMITRA ENRICHED THE WORLDS WITH HIS GOOD DEEDS.

CELEBRATING 50 YEARS

AMAR CHITRA KATHA

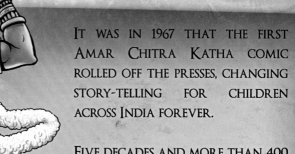

It was in 1967 that the first Amar Chitra Katha comic rolled off the presses, changing story-telling for children across India forever.

Five decades and more than 400 books later, we are still sharing stories from India's rich heritage, primarily because of the love and support shown by readers like yourself.

SO, FROM US TO YOU, HERE'S A BIG

THANK YOU!

AGASTYA

The route to your roots

AGASTYA

He outwitted the Vindhya mountain when, in its pride, it tried to obstruct the natural path of the sun. He drank all the waters of the ocean to expose the wicked Kalkeyas, who hid there after challenging the gods to battle.

Agastya is the most well-known among the Saptarshi. His stories are found not just in the Vedas but are scattered through the Brahmanas and the Puranas as well. These stories are known not only in India but are also a part of S.E. Asian mythology.

Script
Kamala Chandrakant

Illustrations
Ram Waeerkar

Editor
Anant Pai

AGASTYA

SAGE AGASTYA WAS KNOWN IN ALL THE THREE WORLDS FOR HIS WISDOM AND VIRTUE. ONE DAY HE CAME UPON A STRANGE SIGHT IN A FOREST.

WHO COULD THEY BE?

WE ARE YOUR ANCESTORS.

WHY ARE YOU HANGING HERE LIKE THIS?

BECAUSE YOU ARE NOT YET MARRIED. OUR SOULS WILL HAVE NO PEACE TILL WE ARE ASSURED OF THE CONTINUANCE OF OUR LINE.

1

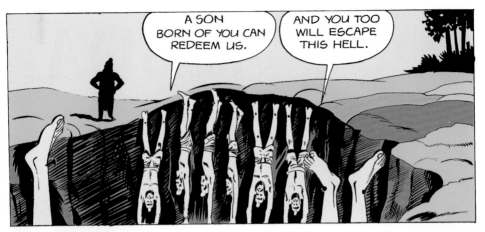

2

AND SO DID AGASTYA CREATE A BEAUTIFUL BABY.

AT THAT TIME THE KING OF VIDARBHA WAS PERFORMING SEVERE PENANCES SO THAT HE MIGHT HAVE A CHILD.

THE CHILD, I HAVE CREATED, SHALL TAKE BIRTH AS THE DAUGHTER OF THIS KING.

A FEW MONTHS LATER THE QUEEN GAVE BIRTH TO A BABY. THE KING WAS OVERJOYED.

O BRAHMANS, MY PENANCES HAVE BEEN FRUITFUL. I HAVE BEEN BLESSED WITH A DAUGHTER.

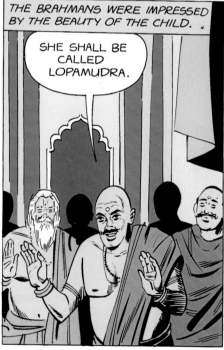

THE BRAHMANS WERE IMPRESSED BY THE BEAUTY OF THE CHILD.

SHE SHALL BE CALLED LOPAMUDRA.

3

LOPAMUDRA GREW UP INTO A BEAUTIFUL AND VIRTUOUS GIRL.

I MUST FIND A WORTHY HUSBAND FOR HER.

MEANWHILE—

LOPAMUDRA MUST NOW BE READY FOR MARRIAGE. I SHALL GO TO HER FATHER AND ASK FOR HER HAND.

HE WENT TO THE KING.

I WISH TO MARRY AND BEGET A SON. WILL YOU GIVE ME YOUR DAUGHTER?

THE KING WAS TROUBLED.

HOW CAN I? BUT I DARE NOT DISPLEASE AGASTYA.

JUST THEN LOPAMUDRA CAME IN.

FATHER, WHY DO YOU HESITATE? I AM WILLING TO MARRY THE GREAT SAGE.

SO SHALL IT BE.

AGASTYA MARRIED LOPAMUDRA.

AFTER THE WEDDING —

LOPAMUDRA, YOUR ROYAL ROBES DO NOT BEFIT A SAGE'S WIFE. DISCARD THEM.

HENCEFORTH I SHALL WEAR ONLY BARK AND SKIN AND RAGS MY LORD.

LOPAMUDRA CAST OFF HER COSTLY ROBES.

COME, LOPAMUDRA. WE WILL GO TO MY HERMITAGE AT GANGOTRI.

BIDDING FAREWELL TO THE SAD PARENTS, AGASTYA LEFT VIDARBHA WITH HIS WIFE.

AT GANGOTRI, LOPAMUDRA HELPED AGASTYA IN HIS SEVERE PENANCES.

DEAR WIFE, YOU WILL SOON BECOME MY EQUAL.

THE DAYS PASSED AND LOPAMUDRA SERVED HER HUSBAND MOST EXCELLENTLY. ONE DAY—

LOPAMUDRA, YOU HAVE PLEASED ME WELL.

MY LORD, I TOO WISH TO BE PLEASED.

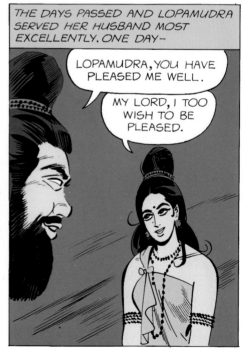

WHAT DO YOU DESIRE?

WE ARE HOUSEHOLDERS. IT IS CERTAINLY NOT WRONG FOR US TO POSSESS WEALTH.

LORD, I WOULD LIKE TO LIVE AS I DID IN MY FATHER'S HOUSE.

THEN I WILL GO OUT IN SEARCH OF WEALTH. WAIT HERE FOR ME.

AGASTYA SET OUT.

I WILL GO TO KING SRUTARVA. HE IS SAID TO BE VERY RICH.

WHEN HE REACHED THE COURT OF SRUTARVA —

O GREAT ONE, WHAT CAN I DO FOR YOU?

I HAVE COME TO YOU FOR WEALTH. GIVE ME WHAT YOU CAN SPARE.

SRUTARVA WAS A GENEROUS. KING. BUT—

I HAVE NO WEALTH TO SPARE. HOWEVER, YOU MAY TAKE AS MUCH AS YOU WANT FROM WHAT I HAVE.

AGASTYA WAS WISE AND VIRTUOUS.

IF I TAKE ANYTHING FROM THIS KING I WILL BE DEPRIVING OTHERS.

HE TURNED TO SRUTARVA.

I CANNOT TAKE ANYTHING FROM YOU. LET US GO AND SEE IF KING BRIHADASTHA CAN HELP ME.

BUT KING BRIHADASTHA TOO HAD NO WEALTH TO SPARE.

PERHAPS KING TRASADASYU WOULD BE ABLE TO HELP. LET US ALL GO TO HIM.

HOWEVER WHEN THEY APPROACHED HIM—

MY REVENUE AND EXPENDITURE ARE EQUAL. BUT I SHALL COME TO YOUR AID IF YOU NEED IT.

NO. I DO NOT WANT TO ACQUIRE WEALTH BY DEPRIVING OTHERS.

THE THREE KINGS LOOKED AT ONE ANOTHER AND SPOKE AS ONE.

THERE IS AN ASURA CALLED ILVALA WHO HAS A GREAT DEAL OF WEALTH. LET US GO TO HIM.

ILVALA WAS A WICKED ASURA. HE HAD A BROTHER CALLED VATAPI. THEY HATED THE BRAHMANS AND HAD VOWED TO KILL AS MANY AS THEY COULD.

VATAPI, I HEAR THAT THE GREAT BRAHMAN SAGE, AGASTYA, IS COMING HERE TODAY. GET READY TO CHANGE YOUR FORM.

I'LL BECOME A GOAT AS USUAL. YOU WILL KILL AND COOK ME...

...AND FEED YOU TO THE BRAHMAN. THEN WHEN I CALL YOU...

...I'LL TEAR HIS STOMACH AND COME RUSHING OUT AND...

...ANOTHER HATED BRAHMAN, THE GREATEST OF THEM ALL, WILL BE DESTROYED.

WHEN AGASTYA AND THE THREE KINGS REACHED ILVALA'S KINGDOM, HE WAS READY TO RECEIVE THEM.

WELCOME, O SAGE, AND YOU, O KINGS. COME, I HAVE COOKED A SPECIAL MEAL IN YOUR HONOUR.

10

THE THREE KINGS WERE ALARMED.

ALAS! I NEVER THOUGHT HE WOULD DARE DO IT TO THE GREAT SAGE.

WE MUST WARN AGASTYA.

WHEN THEY TOLD AGASTYA—

DO NOT WORRY. I WILL BE SAFE.

COME, O GREAT ONE. EAT WITH RELISH.

AGASTYA BEGAN EATING.

HM..M.M! THE TASTIEST MEAL I HAVE EVER EATEN!

AND THE LAST, YOU HATED BRAHMAN.

WHEN AGASTYA HAD EATEN THE LAST MORSEL—

VATAPI, O VATAPI, COME OUT.

BUT—

BuRRRRP

ILVALA BECAME FRANTIC.

VATAPI! O VATAPI! COME OUT. I, ILVALA, AM CALLING YOU.

HA! HA! HA! HA!

HOW CAN HE COME OUT? I HAVE ALREADY DIGESTED HIM.

ILVALA ACCEPTED HIS DEFEAT.

WHY HAVE YOU COME HERE? WHAT CAN I DO FOR YOU?

WE KNOW THAT YOU ARE WEALTHY.

THESE KINGS AND I NEED WEALTH. GIVE US WHAT YOU CAN WITHOUT DEPRIVING ANY OTHER.

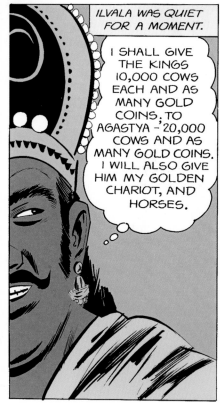

ILVALA WAS QUIET FOR A MOMENT.

I SHALL GIVE THE KINGS 10,000 COWS EACH AND AS MANY GOLD COINS. TO AGASTYA - 20,000 COWS AND AS MANY GOLD COINS. I WILL ALSO GIVE HIM MY GOLDEN CHARIOT, AND HORSES.

THEN HE TURNED TO AGASTYA.

IF YOU CAN GUESS WHAT I INTEND TO GIVE YOU, THAT WILL BE YOURS.

AGASTYA WITH HIS SPIRITUAL INSIGHT EASILY KNEW WHAT ILVALA HAD IN MIND.

YOU INTEND TO GIVE THE KINGS 10,000 COWS EACH AND AS MANY GOLD COINS. AND TO ME, 20,000 COWS, AS MANY COINS, AND YOUR GOLDEN CHARIOT AND HORSES.

YOU HAVE WON THEM ALL. TAKE THEM.

AGASTYA AND THE KINGS MOUNTED THE CHARIOT.

I HAVE HEARD THAT ILVALA'S HORSES ARE THE MOST FLEET-FOOTED IN THE LAND.

ONE DAY, WHILE AGASTYA, LOPAMUDRA AND THEIR SON WERE LIVING AT GANGOTRI...

...THE VINDHYA MOUNTAIN ADDRESSED THE SUN.

O GLORIOUS SUN, YOU GO AROUND MOUNT MERU EVERY DAY AND HONOUR HIM.

I TOO WOULD LIKE TO BE HONOURED IN THE SAME MANNER.

MY PATH HAS BEEN ASSIGNED TO ME SINCE CREATION. I DO NO SPECIAL HONOUR TO MERU.

16

THE SUN'S WORDS ANGERED THE MOUNTAIN.

THEN I SHALL GROW TALLER AND BLOCK YOUR PATH.

SO THE VINDHYA GREW AND GREW.

WHEN THE DEVAS SAW THIS THEY WERE ALARMED.

THIS UNCHECKED GROWTH OF VINDHYA WILL SOON PLUNGE THE EARTH IN DARKNESS.

LET US TRY TO STOP HIM.

THEY WENT TO THE RAPIDLY GROWING MOUNTAIN.

PLEASE DESIST FROM THIS PURSUIT. YOU WILL UPSET THE BALANCE OF CREATION.

THAT IS NOT MY CONCERN.

THE GODS DID NOT KNOW WHAT TO DO. AT LAST—

LET US HASTEN TO AGASTYA. HE IS THE ONLY ONE WHO CAN HELP US.

THE DEVAS WENT TO THE HERMITAGE OF THE SAGE.

WELCOME TO MY HERMITAGE, O DEVAS. WHAT CAN I DO FOR YOU?

O GREAT ONE, WE NEED YOUR HELP.

WHEN THEY HAD TOLD HIM EVERY-THING, AGASTYA REASSURED THEM.

DO NOT WORRY. I WILL DO ALL I CAN. GO IN PEACE.

THE GODS LEFT. AGASTYA TURNED TO LOPAMUDRA.

COME, DEAR ONE. LET US GO AND SEE IF WE CAN STOP HIM.

IT IS OUR DUTY, MY LORD.

THEY WENT TO THE MOUNTAIN.

O GREAT MOUNTAIN, I WISH TO CROSS OVER YOU TO THE SOUTHERN COUNTRY. WAIT TILL I RETURN.

O GREAT SAGE, I WILL STOP INCREASING MY SIZE TILL YOU RETURN FROM THE SOUTH.

SO AGASTYA WITH HIS WIFE AND SON SET OUT FOR THE SOUTH, CROSSING THE VINDHYA.

ONCE THEY HAD REACHED THE OTHER SIDE OF THE MOUNTAIN—

LOPAMUDRA, WE WILL NOT RETURN TO THE NORTH. THEN VINDHYA WILL NEVER BE ABLE TO GROW ANY TALLER.

SO AGASTYA AND HIS FAMILY SETTLED IN THE COUNTRY SOUTH OF THE VINDHYA MOUNTAIN.

THE KALKEYAS, A GROUP OF ASURAS, WERE BECOMING A NUISANCE TO THE THREE WORLDS. THE DEVAS WERE IN TROUBLE.

THE KALKEYAS ARE NOW ATTACKING OUR CITIES.

THEY DARE TO · BECAUSE VRITRA LEADS THEM.

HE MUST BE DESTROYED.

LET US APPROACH BRAHMA FOR HELP.

SO THE DEVAS LED BY INDRA, THEIR KING, WENT TO BRAHMA. BRAHMA KNEW WHY THEY HAD COME.

GO TO THE GREAT SAGE DADHICHI AND ASK HIM FOR HIS BONES. TAKE THE BONES TO TWASHTRI AND ASK HIM TO MAKE A WEAPON FOR YOU WITH THEM.

WITH THAT WEAPON YOU, INDRA, WILL KILL VRITRA.

THE DEVAS GOT THE BONES FROM DADHICHI AND WENT TO TWASHTRI.

I WILL MAKE THE WEAPON VAJRA FOR YOU.

WHEN HE FINISHED HE TURNED TO INDRA.

TAKE THIS AND DESTROY THE ENEMY.

CONFIDENT OF VICTORY, INDRA AND THE DEVAS ATTACKED VRITRA AND THE KALKEYAS.

BUT BEFORE THEY COULD ADVANCE, THE KALKEYAS RUSHED AT THEM WITH THEIR MACES.

NOT EXPECTING THIS THE DEVAS BROKE THEIR RANKS...

...AND FLED IN PANIC.

INDRA LOST HEART.

WHAT SHALL I DO? IN SPITE OF BRAHMA'S PROMISE THE DEVAS HAVE DESERTED ME.

HE TURNED TO VISHNU FOR HELP.

DO NOT FEAR. I SHALL GIVE YOU A PORTION OF MY MIGHT.

WHEN VRITRA LEARNT OF THE HELP OBTAINED BY INDRA, HE ROARED IN ANGER.

COME, O LEADER OF THE DEVAS. TASTE OF MY MIGHT TOO!

INDRA WITH HIS NEWLY ACQUIRED STRENGTH HURLED THE VAJRA AT HIM.

THE VAJRA FOUND ITS MARK.

BOOM

THE GREAT ASURA FELL DEAD.

THUD

WHEN THE DEVAS HEARD THE NEWS—

VRITRA IS DEAD. NOW WE CAN VANQUISH THE KALKEYAS.

THEY CHARGED AT THE HAPLESS ASURAS.

WE ARE DOOMED. THERE IS NO ONE TO LEAD US.

PANIC-STRICKEN, THE ASURAS FLED, AWAY FROM THE FIELD...

RUN! RUN!

...INTO THE DEEP OCEAN.

THEY WILL NOT FIND US HERE.

RID OF THE KALKEYAS THE DEVAS REJOICED.

WE MAY NOW LIVE IN PEACE.

MEANWHILE THE KALKEYAS ASSEMBLED IN THEIR UNDERWATER HOME AND PLANNED REVENGE.

WE MUST KILL ALL GOOD MEN ON EARTH. THEIR DEATH WILL DESTROY THE WHOLE UNIVERSE.

WE MUST DO OUR WORK BY NIGHT. WE WILL NOT BE FOUND OUT.

AND THE KALKEYAS BEGAN THEIR WORK OF DESTRUCTION.

EooEoAH!

WARRIORS AND HEROES WENT IN SEARCH OF THE MURDERERS, BUT COULD NOT FIND THEM.

WHO COULD THEY BE? WHERE DO THEY VANISH?

WHERE COULD THEY BE HIDING? WE HAVE SEARCHED EVERYWHERE.

INDRA AND THE DEVAS, WERE PERTURBED.

LET US GO TO VISHNU FOR HELP.

THEY WENT TO HIM.

LORD, YOU HAVE ALWAYS COME TO OUR AID WHEN WE NEEDED YOU.

WHAT IS IT NOW?

THE GOOD MEN ON EARTH ARE BEING DESTROYED.

WE DO NOT KNOW WHO THE CULPRITS ARE.

THE DESTRUCTION OF GOOD MEN WILL MEAN THE END OF HEAVEN ITSELF.

VISHNU TURNED TO INDRA.

WHEN VRITRA WAS KILLED BY YOU, THE KALKEYAS FLED INTO THE OCEAN BED TO SAVE THEIR LIVES. THEY ARE THE CULPRITS.

THEY CANNOT BE KILLED AS THEY HAVE TAKEN SHELTER UNDER THE SEA.

WHAT SHOULD WE DO?

YOU MUST FIND OUT SOME MEANS TO DRY UP THE OCEAN.

BUT WHO CAN ACCOMPLISH SUCH A TASK?

WHO ELSE, BUT AGASTYA!

THE HOPEFUL DEVAS WENT TO AGASTYA.

GREAT ONE, YOU CONSUMED THE EVIL VATAPI. YOU PREVENTED VINDHYA FROM PLUNGING THE WORLD IN ETERNAL DARKNESS.

SO WE HAVE COME TO YOU FOR HELP.

WHAT DO YOU WANT ME TO DO?

WE WANT YOU TO DRINK THE OCEAN. THEN WE SHALL BE ABLE TO KILL OUR ENEMIES, THE EVIL KALKEYAS.

I SHALL DO WHAT YOU DESIRE AS IT WILL BENEFIT THE WORLD.

WHEN THEY REACHED THE OCEAN—

ARRAY YOURSELVES FOR WAR WHILE I DRINK THE OCEAN.

AND AGASTYA BEGAN DRINKING THE OCEAN.

BUT THE KALKEYAS WERE UNABLE TO WITHSTAND THE ONSLAUGHT...

...AND WERE SOON VANQUISHED.

AGASTYA WATCHED WITH HAPPINESS THE VICTORY OF THE DEVAS.

MY TASK IS ACCOMPLISHED. I MAY NOW GO BACK TO MY PENANCES. PEACE BE WITH YOU.

THUS ONCE MORE THE JUST AND WISE SON OF MITRA AND VARUNA SUPPRESSED EVIL AND PROTECTED THE GOOD.

The route to your roots

PARASHURAMA

It was a time when the earth was ravaged with violence and bloodshed. The Kshatriya kings had forgotten their duty to rule with compassion. Instead, they subdued the people by unleashing a reign of brutal terror. At such a time the sixth incarnation of Vishnu was born. Parashurama, axe-wielding warrior-saint, strode across the age to destroy evil and liberate good.

Script
Kamala Chandrakant

Illustrations
Madhu Powle

Editor
Anant Pai

PARASHURAMA

PARASHURAMA WAS BORN THE SON OF RISHI JAMADAGNI AND RENUKA. BUT IT WAS A BIRTH UNDER STRANGE CIRCUMSTANCES.

HIS GREAT-GRANDFATHER, GADHI, WAS A GOOD KING.

WE ARE FORTUNATE THAT OUR KING IS STRONG AND KIND.

YES. AS LONG AS HE RULES, WE NEED FEAR NONE.

GADHI HAD A DAUGHTER CALLED SATYAVATI, BUT NO SON.

ONE DAY BHRIGU'S SON, RICHIKA SAW HER.

HOW BEAUTIFUL, PURE AND GOOD SHE LOOKS! I WOULD MARRY HER.

2

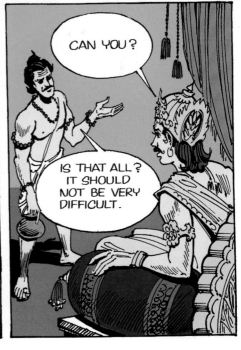

3

SO RICHIKA GAVE GADHI THE THOUSAND BROWN HORSES...

...AND WAS MARRIED TO SATYAVATI.

ONE DAY BHRIGU CAME TO VISIT HIS SON AND DAUGHTER-IN-LAW.

THEY LOOKED AFTER HIS NEEDS WITH AFFECTION.

I AM INDEED FORTUNATE IN MY CHILDREN.

BHRIGU WAS PLEASED.

OBEDIENT AND DUTIFUL DAUGHTER-IN-LAW, I AM WILLING TO GRANT YOU ANY BOON YOU ASK OF ME.

FATHER, GIVE ME A SON AND A BROTHER.

YOU SHALL HAVE BOTH.

THEN HE TOOK SATYAVATI ASIDE.

HERE ARE TWO POTS OF SACRED RICE AND MILK. THIS ONE IS FOR YOU...

... AND THAT ONE FOR YOUR MOTHER.

WHEN BHRIGU LEFT, SATYAVATI PICKED THE POTS AND ALONG WITH HER HUSBAND WENT TO HER MOTHER

WHEN SHE REACHED —

MOTHER! MOTHER! I HAVE TWO POTS OF SACRED RICE AND MILK, WHICH WILL GIVE US A MIGHTY SON EACH.

YOUR MARRIAGE TO RICHIKA HAS INDEED BROUGHT US GOOD FORTUNE.

BUT HER MOTHER TOOK THE POT MEANT FOR SATYAVATI AND...

...SATYAVATI TOOK THE ONE MEANT FOR HER MOTHER.

SAGE BHRIGU IN HIS SPIRITUAL VISION SAW THE EXCHANGE.

ALAS, MY CHILD! YOU DID NOT HEED MY INSTRUCTIONS CAREFULLY.

NOW, YOUR MOTHER'S SON THOUGH A KSHATRIYA, WILL TAKE TO THE LIFE OF AN ASCETIC.

AND YOUR SON THOUGH A BRAHMANA, WILL BECOME A WARRIOR.

SATYAVATI BEGAN PLEADING WITH BHRIGU.

O REVERED SIRE, LET MY GRANDSON BE SUCH BUT NOT MY SON.

BHRIGU WAS MOVED BY HER ENTREATIES.

SO BE IT, MY CHILD. SO BE IT.

IN DUE TIME SATYAVATI HAD A SON.

WE SHALL CALL HIM JAMDAGNI.

AS JAMADAGNI GREW UP, HIS DEVOTION TO THE STUDY OF THE VEDAS ALSO INCREASED AND HE SOON MASTERED THEM.

NOW I SHALL ENTER THE LIFE OF A HOUSEHOLDER. I AM READY FOR IT.

SO HE MARRIED THE CHASTE RENUKA.

MOST OF THE KSHATRIYAS OF THOSE DAYS WERE VICIOUS. THEY WERE BECOMING A MENACE AND A BURDEN TO MOTHER EARTH. THE WORST OF THEM WAS KARTAVIRYA ARJUNA, THE 1000-ARMED KING OF THE HAIHAYA TRIBE.

MEN, WOMEN AND CHILDREN TREMBLED WITH FEAR WHENEVER KARTAVIRYA ARJUNA RODE INTO A CITY IN HIS INVINCIBLE GOLDEN CHARIOT.

RUN! RUN! KARTAVIRYA ARJUNA IS HERE!

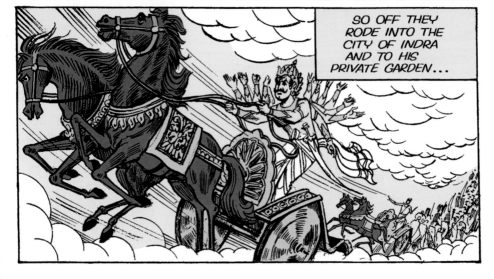

AS SOON AS THE SAGES HAD LEFT, INDRA ENTERED.

LORD VISHNU, KARTAVIRYA ARJUNA NOW COVETS THE WEALTH OF THE VERY HEAVENS. HE MUST BE DESTROYED.

I KNOW.

I WILL TAKE AN AVATAR ON EARTH AS A BRAHMANA WITH UNUSUAL PHYSICAL PROWESS AND OVERPOWER HIM.

MEANWHILE FIVE SONS WERE BORN TO RENUKA AND JAMADAGNI.

THE FIFTH AND YOUNGEST WAS RAMA WHO WAS REALLY VISHNU REBORN TO FULFIL HIS PROMISE TO INDRA AND THE SAGES.

AS A CHILD RAMA WAS FOND OF PHYSICAL EXERCISE AND...

ENOUGH, RAMA. I GIVE UP. YOU ARE STRONGER THAN I AM.

...PLAYING WITH WEAPONS.

RAMA SOON GREW UP INTO A STURDY YOUTH. ONE DAY—

FATHER, I WISH TO GO TO THE GANDHAMADANA MOUNTAINS AND BY AUSTERE PENANCES GAIN LORD SHIVA'S FAVOUR.

GO IF YOU MUST, MY SON. YOU HAVE MY BLESSINGS.

RAMA WENT AND SAT IN MEDITATION AND UNDERWENT SEVERE PENANCES.

AT LAST SHIVA APPEARED TO HIM.

YOU HAVE PLEASED ME BY YOUR DEVOTION. WHAT IS IT THAT YOU DESIRE?

I HAVE SET MY HEART ON THE FIERY AXE, THE POWERFUL PARASHU.

AS YOU DESERVE, YOU SHALL HAVE IT. NO WARRIOR ON EARTH SHALL SURPASS YOU.

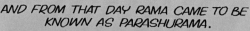

AND FROM THAT DAY RAMA CAME TO BE KNOWN AS PARASHURAMA.

TAKING HIS AXE, PARASHU-RAMA RETURNED TO HIS FATHER'S ASHRAM.

JAMADAGNI WAS OVERJOYED TO SEE HIM.

MY SON, I AM GLAD YOU HAVE RETURNED. NOW YOU ARE THERE TO DO IT.

DO WHAT FATHER?

KILL YOUR MOTHER! SHE HAS SINNED.

FATHER, IT IS MY DUTY TO OBEY YOU.

IT IS WELL YOU DO. YOUR BROTHERS REFUSED. I HAVE CURSED THEM WITH MADNESS.

PARASHURAMA, WITH ONE BLOW OF HIS AXE, KILLED HIS MOTHER.

YOUR UNQUESTIONING OBEDIENCE PLEASES ME. ASK ANY BOON AND IT SHALL BE YOURS.

THIS WAS WHAT PARASHURAMA WAS WAITING FOR.

RESTORE MY MOTHER'S LIFE AND LOVE HER AS BEFORE. GIVE MY BROTHERS BACK THEIR SENSES. AND GIVE ME EVERLASTING LIFE.

EXACTLY AS I HAD FORESEEN!

SO BE IT

JAMADAGNI WAS ONLY TOO GLAD TO GRANT HIM HIS BOONS.

16

MEANWHILE KARTAVIRYA ARJUNA CONTINUED IN HIS TYRANNY. ONE DAY WHILE PACING ARROGANTLY ON THE SEASHORE, HE BEGAN SHOOTING ARROWS INTO THE WATERS OF THE OCEAN.

A VOICE FROM THE OCEAN STOPPED HIM.

PLEASE DO NOT HARM THE CREATURES THAT LIVE WITHIN ME. I SHALL DO WHATEVER YOU ASK OF ME BUT PLEASE SPARE THEM.

I WILL IF YOU ANSWER THIS QUESTION. IS THERE A MAN WHO CAN RIVAL ME?

YES. PARASHURAMA, THE SON OF JAMADAGNI. HE IS MORE THAN YOUR EQUAL.

18

THAT NIGHT THE SONS OF ARJUNA STOLE THE CALF AND MADE OFF WITH IT.

IN THE MORNING WHEN JAMADAGNI CAME OUT OF THE ASHRAM —

ALAS! KARTAVIRYA ARJUNA HAS REPAID OUR HOSPITALITY BY STEALING YOUR CALF.

JUST THEN PARASHURAMA RETURNED. HE SAW THEM.

WHAT HAS HAPPENED TO HER, FATHER? WHY IS SHE SO SAD? WHERE IS HER CALF? WHY ARE THEY SEPARATED?

JAMADAGNI TOLD HIM THE WHOLE STORY.

I SHALL KILL HIM AND REDEEM YOUR CALF!

THEN PARASHURAMA TOOK HIS AXE AND RUSHED TO THE PALACE OF KARTAVIRYA ARJUNA.

WHEN HE SAW THE HELPLESS CALF, HE COULD NOT CONTROL HIS ANGER. HE RUSHED INTO KARTAVIRYA ARJUNA'S BEDROOM.

A DREADFUL COMBAT ENSUED IN WHICH PARASHURAMA HACKED OFF EACH ONE OF KARTAVIRYA ARJUNA'S THOUSAND ARMS AND...

...SLEW HIM.

THEN PICKING THE FRIGHTENED CALF GENTLY IN HIS ARMS...

...HE MADE HIS WAY BACK TO HIS FATHER'S ASHRAM.

FATHER! FATHER! I HAVE KILLED HIM! THE VILLAIN WHO STOLE OUR INNOCENT CALF.

THEN THEY WENT TO THE COW AND –

GENTLE MOTHER, I HAVE BROUGHT BACK YOUR CALF FOR YOU.

PARASHURAMA, I AM PROUD OF YOU.

THE FIREWOOD IS EXHAUSTED. I SHALL GO TO THE FOREST AND CUT SOME FOR YOU.

IN THE MEANWHILE –

ALAS! HE IS DEAD AND THE CALF IS MISSING.

NONE OTHER THAN PARASHURAMA COULD BE THE MURDERER.

THEY WERE FURIOUS.

HE SHALL BE AVENGED! COME, LET US SEEK OUT THE MURDERER.

THEY MOUNTED THEIR CHARIOTS AND CHARGED OUT OF THE PALACE.

WHEN THEY REACHED THE ASHRAM, JAMADAGNI WAS DEEP IN MEDITATION.

PARASHURAMA IS NOT TO BE SEEN ANYWHERE.

LET US KILL HIS FATHER THEN.

THAT'S RIGHT. HE KILLED OUR FATHER. DIDN'T HE?

THEY ATTACKED JAMADAGNI AND SHOT ARROWS AT HIM FROM ALL DIRECTIONS.

THEY LEFT HIM DYING AND RODE AWAY.

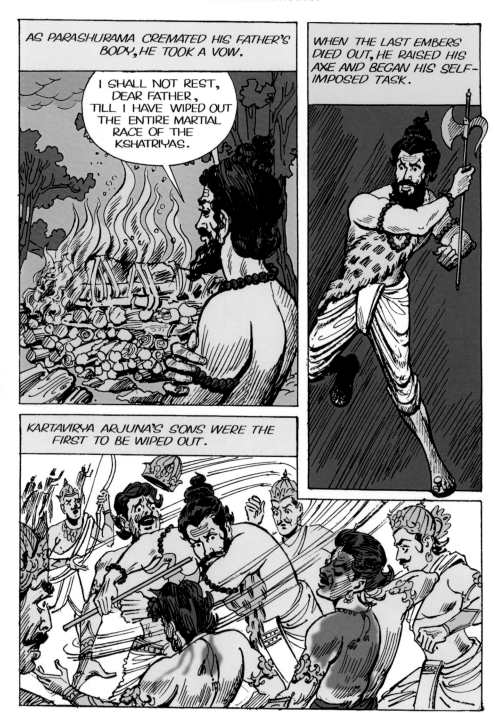

AS PARASHURAMA CREMATED HIS FATHER'S BODY, HE TOOK A VOW.

I SHALL NOT REST, DEAR FATHER, TILL I HAVE WIPED OUT THE ENTIRE MARTIAL RACE OF THE KSHATRIYAS.

WHEN THE LAST EMBERS DIED OUT, HE RAISED HIS AXE AND BEGAN HIS SELF-IMPOSED TASK.

KARTAVIRYA ARJUNA'S SONS WERE THE FIRST TO BE WIPED OUT.

THEN ONE BY ONE HE MASSACRED ALL THE KSHATRIYAS ON EARTH.

BUT EACH TIME HE KILLED ONE LOT, THEIR SONS WOULD SPRING UP.

I SHALL FIGHT TILL NOT A SINGLE ONE OF YOU IS LEFT. MY FATHER HAS GRANTED ME EVERLASTING LIFE.

THUS PARASHURAMA PATIENTLY CONTINUED WIPING OUT TWENTY-ONE GENERATIONS OF KSHATRIYAS.

BUT ALAS! HE KILLED WITHOUT DISCRIMINATION BOTH THE EVIL AND THE GOOD KSHATRIYAS.

I HAVE HARMED NONE. MY SUBJECTS ARE HAPPY. WHY DO YOU WANT TO KILL ME AND DEPRIVE THEM OF MY PROTECTION?

BUT PARASHURAMA WAS RELENTLESS.

ONE OF YOUR CASTE MURDERED MY FATHER WHILE HE WAS DEFENCELESS. SO YOU SHALL DIE.

SOON THERE WERE NO STRONG GOOD MEN TO PROTECT THE GOOD ON EARTH.

ALAS! OUR KING IS KILLED, AND THERE IS NONE TO PROTECT US.

SHUDRAS AND VAISHYAS HAVE NO REGARD FOR BRAHMANAS AND THEIR WOMEN.

MOTHER EARTH FELT THAT IT WAS TIME TO INTERVENE.

I SHALL APPROACH SAGE KASHYAPA.